Praying

Meeting God in Daily Life

Lyn Klug

Augsburg Fortress, Minneapolis

Contents

INTERSECTIONS
Small Group Series

Praying
Meeting God in Daily Life

Developed in cooperation with the Division for Congregational Ministries

George S. Johnson, series introduction
David W. Anderson and Carolyn F. Lystig, editors
The Wells Group, series design
Betts Anderson/Unicorn Stock Photos, cover photo

Scripture quotations are from New Revised Standard Version Bible, copyright 1989 Division of Christian Education of the National Council of the Churches of Christ in the United States of America. Used by permission.

        6 7 8 9 0 1 2 3 4 5 6 7 8 9

Introduction

Statistics show that more people are praying more—or want to. But people also have questions, doubts, and reservations about God and prayer.

- Who is God?
- Can prayer and a modern worldview coexist?
- Is seeking personal benefits from God another form of materialism and self-interest?

Praying people

Our goal is to become praying people who experience the effects of God in our lives. The goal of prayer is not to dictate to God what we need to experience a satisfying life. However, the concerns of our lives need to be taken seriously. If the issues of our own life experiences and contemporary society are not present in our prayer, why pray?

What do you want?

Jesus asked sick people, "What do you want me to do for you?" Our answer is probably the same as theirs. We want to be well, to live well, to be of use in a world that needs us. Those who give the most tend to pray the most. Their vision and their energy come from beyond themselves, through prayer.

Ordinary people

Stories of the great believers' total dependence on prayer, or stories of dramatic answers to prayers, or even a good retreat leader's personal experience of prayer are often not the best place to begin.

It may be more helpful to begin with ordinary people who have ordinary experiences to share, and with many of the same doubts and questions that most of us have.

Neither are creeds, doctrines, or Bible study a substitute for our own experience.

- Who is God for me?
- How does the truth about God become true in me, and for me?
- What role does Jesus play in my life?

Simple guidelines

Because we are unique people with unique personalities and needs, we need to find our own best ways of praying. A few simple guidelines will help.

- Your ways of praying will evolve as you go. Trust your own experience.
- Take every opportunity to learn—from books, tapes, groups, other people, church.
- Don't compare yourself with anyone. Take what you need and leave the rest. You may come back to it later.
- Techniques and methods are not ends in themselves, but means to a closer relationship with God. As you continue in prayer, some ways of praying will become natural and permanent for you.

Why in a group?

Why explore such a personal thing in a group? *First,* personal does not mean private. Christianity has always included both communal and personal prayer. There is a depth and power to prayer in a group that can also assist our personal prayer.

Second, we need a place to be understood and to share our experience, ideas, and questions with others. We need encouragement to keep on, to keep it simple, and to be ourselves. We can find a great sense of belonging and connection, a "coming home" among people who want to pray.

We will be addressing such questions as these in the group:

- When is it good to pray? How?
- Who are we praying to?
- What happens?
- Can we expect anything for sure?
- What should we pray about?
- How do we pray for others?
- Does it affect them?
- Do we have to use words?
- How does God speak to us?
- How can we best pray with others?

If you feel like a complete beginner, you are in good company. If you have a lot of experience in prayer, you can reassure others that everyone is always a beginner.

In our culture, we expect so much, so fast. Someone recently remarked that prayer was too "old fashioned" and too "time consuming," that we need some "'90s prayer." I'm not sure what '90s prayer would be, but I'm sure that centuries of Jewish and Christian ways of praying are good for '90s people.

Facilitator helps

Leading prayer

This candle in the margin refers you back to this page for help in leading prayer exercises.

Before each prayer exercise, have people put books and journals away, close their eyes, and find a comfortable position on their chair or the floor.

Move through the prayer exercise *slowly*, reading each section of directions out loud. Pause (indicated by . . .) long enough between each section to do the exercise.

End each exercise by saying "Amen" quietly. Then give people a moment to refocus their attention to the larger group.

People can feel left out or inferior because they do not have the same kinds of experiences as others. Reassure them that God meets us in very different ways, and that the effects of prayer have nothing to do with certain experiences.

Sometimes, people's responses to the prayer exercise will need to be simply *heard,* not discussed by others. Help the group distinguish between sharing and discussing an experience.

For some rituals or prayer exercises, turn off most lights and leave only candles. People can relax and settle down faster in dimmer light.

If you are leading all the sessions, ask if others will lead some prayer exercises so you can just pray.

Sensitivity

Make it very clear that no one has to do any exercise or share any thought or experience that they would prefer not to. Help people feel comfortable about keeping silent.

Encourage questions. They may be more real and honest than answers. Try not to just answer someone's question, but instead get to the reason behind the question—convictions, doubts, experience, fears, obstacles, observations. This can be helpful to everyone.

Let the group help decide whether to answer questions in journals, as a group, in groups of three or four, or in pairs. They will gain a sense of what they prefer for different types of question

When a series of Bible passages is to be studied, it may help to locate and mark the individual texts in one or more Bibles in advance. This will save time and benefit those not familiar with the books of the Bible.

SMALL GROUP SERIES

Welcome into the family of those who are part of small groups! Intersections Small Group Series will help you and other members of your group build relationships and discover ways to connect the Christian faith with your everyday life.

This book is prepared for those who want to make a difference in this world, who want to grow in their Christian faith, as well as for those who are beginning to explore the Christian faith. The information in this introduction to the Intersections small group experience can help your group make the most out of your time together.

Biblical encouragement

"Do not be conformed to this world, but be transformed by the renewing of your minds, so that you may discern what is the will of God—what is good and acceptable and perfect" (Romans 12:2).

Small groups provide an atmosphere where the Holy Spirit can transform lives. As you share your life stories and learn together, God's Spirit can work to enlighten and direct you.

Strength is provided to face the pressures to conform to forces and influences that are opposed to what is "good and acceptable and perfect." To "be transformed" is an ongoing experience of God's grace as we take up the cross and follow Jesus. Changed lives happen as we live in community with one another. Small groups encourage such change and growth.

What is a small group?

A number of definitions and descriptions of the small group ministry experience exist throughout the church. Roberta Hestenes, a Presbyterian pastor and author, defines a small group as an intentional face-to-face gathering of three to twelve people who meet regularly with the common purpose of discovering and growing in the possibilities of the abundant life.

Whatever definition you use, the following characteristics are important.

Small—Seven to ten people is ideal so that everyone can be heard and no one's voice is lost. More than 12 members makes genuine caring difficult.

Intentional—Commitment to the group is a high priority.

Personal—Sharing experiences and insights is more important than mastering content.

Conversational—Leaders that facilitate conversation, rather than teach, are the key to encouraging participation.

Friendly—Having a warm, accepting, non-judgmental atmosphere is essential.

Christ-centered—The small group experience is biblically based, related to the real world, and founded on Christ.

Features of Intersections Small Group Series

A small group model

A number of small group ministry models exist. Most models include three types of small groups:

- *Discipleship groups*—where people gather to grow in Christian faith and life;

- *Support and recovery groups*—which focus on special interests, concerns, or needs; and

- *Ministry groups*—which have a task-oriented focus.

Intersections Small Group Series presently offers material for discipleship groups and support and recovery groups.

For discipleship groups, this series offers a variety of courses with Bible study at the center. What makes a discipleship group different from traditional group Bible studies? In discipleship groups, members bring their life experience to the exploration of the biblical material.

For support and recovery groups, Intersections Small Group Series offers topical material to assist group members in dealing with issues related to their common experience, hurt, or interest. An extra section of facilitator helps in the back of the book will assist leaders of support and recovery groups to anticipate and prepare for special circumstances and needs that may arise as group members explore a topic.

Ministry groups can benefit from an environment that includes prayer, biblical reflection, and relationship building, in addition to their task focus.

Four essentials

Prayer, personal sharing, biblical reflection, and a group ministry task are part of each time you gather. These are all important for Christian community to be experienced. Each of the six chapter themes in each book includes:

- Short prayers to open and close your time together.

- Carefully worded questions to make personal sharing safe, non-threatening, and voluntary.

- A biblical base from which to understand and discover the power and grace of God. God's Word is the compass that keeps the group on course.

- A group ministry task to encourage both individuals and the group as a whole to find ways to put faith into action.

Flexibility

Each book contains six chapter themes that may be covered in six sessions or easily extended for groups that meet for a longer period of time. Each chapter theme is organized around two to three main topics with supplemental material to make it easily adaptable to your small group's needs. You need not use all the material. Most themes will work well for 1½- to 2-hour sessions, but a variety of scheduling options is possible.

Bible based

Each of the six chapter themes in the book includes one or more Bible texts printed in its entirety from the New Revised Standard Version of the Bible. This makes it easy for all group members to read and learn from the same text. Participants will be encouraged through questions, with exercises, and by other group members to address biblical texts in the context of their own lives.

User friendly

The material is prepared in such a way that it is easy to follow, practical, and does not require a professional to lead it. Designating one to be the facilitator to guide the group is important, but there is no requirement for this person to be theologically trained or an expert in the course topic. Many times options are given so that no one will feel forced into any set way of responding.

Group goals and process

1. Creating a group covenant or contract for your time together will be important. During your first meeting, discuss these important characteristics of all small groups and decide how your group will handle them.

Confidentiality—Agreeing that sensitive issues that are shared remain in the group.

Regular attendance—Agreeing to make meetings a top priority.

Non-judgmental behavior—Agreeing to confess one's own shortcomings, if appropriate, not those of others, and not giving advice unless asked for it.

Prayer and support—Being sensitive to one another, listening, becoming a caring community.

Accountability—Being responsible to each other and open to change.

Items in your covenant should be agreed upon by all members. Add to the group covenant as you go along. Space to record key aspects is included in the back of this book. See page 60.

2. Everyone is responsible for the success of the group, but do arrange to have one facilitator who can guide the group process each time you meet.

The facilitator is not a teacher or healer. Teaching, learning, and healing happen from the group experience. The facilitator is more of a shepherd who leads the flock to where they can feed and drink and feel safe.

Remember, an important goal is to experience genuine love and community in a Christ-centered atmosphere. To help make this happen, the facilitator encourages active listening and honest sharing. This person allows the material to facilitate opportunities for self-awareness and interaction with others.

Leadership is shared in a healthy group, but the facilitator is the one designated to set the pace, keep the group focused, and enable the members to support and care for each other.

People need to sense trust and freedom as the group develops; therefore, avoid "shoulds" or "musts" in your group.

3. Taking on a group ministry task can help members of your group balance personal growth with service to others.

In your first session, identify ways your group can offer help to others within the congregation or in your surrounding community. Take time at each meeting to do or arrange for that ministry task. Many times it is in the doing that we discover what we believe or how God is working in our lives.

4. Starting or continuing a personal action plan offers a way to address personal needs that you become aware of in your small group experience.

For example, you might want to spend more time in conversation with a friend or spouse. Your action plan might state, "I plan to visit with Terry two times before our next small group meeting."

If you decide to pursue a personal action plan, consider sharing it with your small group. Your group can be helpful in at least three ways: by giving support; helping to define the plan in realistic, measurable ways; and offering a source to whom you can be accountable.

5. Prayer is part of small group fellowship. There is great power in group prayer, but not everyone feels free to offer spontaneous prayer. That's okay.

Learning to pray aloud takes time and practice. If you feel uncomfortable, start with simple and short prayers. And remember to pray for other members between sessions.

Use page 61 in the back of this book to note prayer requests made by group members.

6. Consider using a journal to help reflect on your experiences and insights between meeting times.

Writing about feelings, ideas, and questions can be one way to express yourself; plus it helps you remember what so often gets lost with time.

The "Daily Walk" component includes material that can get your journaling started. This, of course, is up to you and need not be done on any regular schedule. Even doing it once a week can be time well spent.

How to use this book

The material provided for each session is organized around some key components. If you are the facilitator for your small group, be sure to read this section carefully.

The facilitator's role is to establish a hospitable atmosphere and set a tone that encourages participants to share, reflect, and listen to each other. Some important practical things can help make this happen.

- Whenever possible meet in homes. Be sure to provide clear directions about how to get there.
- Use name tags for several sessions.
- Place the chairs in a circle and close enough for everyone to hear and feel connected.
- Be sure everyone has access to a book; preparation will pay off.

Welcoming

The physical setting for a prayer group is very important. Try to use a room with a warm cozy atmosphere, comfortable chairs (or pillows), and incandescent lamps that can be turned off. There should be reasonable quiet and no interruptions.

Each week, provide (you or group members) a center to the circle on the floor or on a low table—candles, stones, flowers, leaves, bowls of water with floating candles, icons or pictures of people from around the world arranged on a scarf or tablecloth.

In addition to name tags, try to get the people in the group to learn each other's names by various means—they need to feel comfortable with each other as soon as possible. People will need journals. Using an inexpensive $8\frac{1}{2}$ x 11" spiral-bound notebook avoids the need for a table to write on. Above all, slow down and relax. If you set a peaceful tone, people will appreciate being there.

Focus

Each of the six chapter themes in this book has a brief focus statement. Read it aloud. It will give everyone a sense of the direction for each session and provide some boundaries so that people will not feel lost or frustrated trying to cover everything. The focus also connects the theme to the course topic.

Community building

This opening activity is crucial to a relaxed, friendly atmosphere. It will prepare the ground for gradual group development. Two "Community Building" options are provided under each theme. With the facilitator giving his or her response to the questions first, others are free to follow.

One purpose for this section is to allow everyone to participate as he or she responds to non-threatening questions. The activity serves as a check-in time when participants are invited to share how things are going or what is new.

Make this time light and fun; remember, humor is a welcome gift. Use 15 to 20 minutes for this activity in your first few sessions and keep the entire group together.

During your first meeting, encourage group members to write down names and phone numbers (when appropriate) of the other members, so people can keep in touch. Use page 59 for this purpose.

Discovery

This component focuses on exploring the theme for your time together, using material that is read, and questions and exercises that encourage sharing of personal insights and experiences.

Reading material includes a Bible text with supplemental passages and commentary written by the topic writer. Have volunteers read the Bible texts aloud. Read the commentary aloud only when it seems helpful. The main passage to be used is printed so that everyone operates from a common translation and sees the text.

"A Further Look" is included in some places to give you additional study material if time permits. Use it to explore related passages and questions. Be sure to have your own Bible handy.

Questions and exercises related to the theme will invite personal sharing and storytelling. Keep in mind that as you listen to each other's stories, you are inspired to live more fully in the grace and will of God. Such exchanges make Christianity relevant and transformation more likely to happen. Caring relationships are key to clarifying one's beliefs. Sharing personal experiences and insights is what makes the small group spiritually satisfying.

Most people are open to sharing their life stories, especially if they're given permission to do so and they know someone will actively listen. Starting with the facilitator's response usually works best. On some occasions you may want to break the group into units of three or four persons to explore certain questions. When you reconvene, relate your experience to the whole group. The phrase "Explore and Relate," which appears occasionally in the margin, refers to this recommendation. Encourage couples to separate for this smaller group activity. Appoint someone to start the discussion.

Wrap-up

Plan your schedule so that there will be enough time for wrapping up. This time can include work on your group ministry task, review of key discoveries during your time together, identifying personal and prayer concerns, closing prayers, and the Lord's Prayer.

The facilitator can help the group identify and plan its ministry task. Introduce the idea and decide on your group ministry task during "Wrap-up" time in the first session. Tasks need not be grandiose. Activities might include:

- Ministry in your community, such as "adopting" a food shelf, clothes closet, or homeless shelter; sponsoring equipment, food, or clothing drives; or sending members to staff the shelter.

- Ministry to members of the congregation, such as writing notes to those who are ill or bereaved.

- Congregational tasks where volunteers are always needed, such as serving refreshments during the fellowship time after worship, stuffing envelopes for a church mailing, or taking responsibility for altar preparations for one month.

Depending upon the task, you can use part of each meeting time to carry out or plan the task.

In the "Wrap-up," allow time for people to share insights and encouragements and to voice special prayer requests. Just to mention someone who needs prayer is a form of prayer. The "Wrap-up" time may include a brief worship experience with candles, prayers, and singing. You might form a circle and hold hands. Silence can be effective. If you use the Lord's Prayer in your group, select the version that is known in your setting. There is space on page 62 to record the version your group uses. Another closing prayer is also printed on page 62. Before you go, ask members to pray for one another during the week. Remember also any special concerns or prayer requests.

Daily walk

Seven Bible readings and a thought, prayer, and verse for the journey related to the material just discussed are provided for those who want to keep the theme before them between sessions. These brief readings may be used for devotional time. Some group members may want to memorize selected passages. The Bible readings can also be used for supplemental study by the group if needed. Prayer for other group members can also be part of this time of personal reflection.

A word of encouragement

No material is ever complete or perfect for every situation or group. Creativity and imagination will be important gifts for the facilitator to bring to each theme. Keep in mind that it is in community that we are challenged to grow in Jesus Christ. Together we become what we could not become alone. It is God's plan that it be so.

For additional resources and ideas see *Starting Small Groups—and Keeping Them Going* (Minneapolis: Augsburg Fortress, 1995).

1   Who Is God?

Focus

Prayer does not depend on a clear or complete understanding of God. As we pray, we expand our ways of experiencing God's grace, love, and guidance.

Community building

Small groups can include clubs, classes, study or support groups, groups of friends, sports teams—any group that meets regularly.

For setting small group goals, see page 7.

- Take a few minutes to reflect upon the following sentences. Then share your thoughts with each other.

  a. My first experience with a small group was . . .

  b. The small groups I belong to now are . . .

List your goals and commitments in the appendix on page 60 for future reference.

  c. The best small group I ever participated in was . . .

  d. A group is most helpful to me when . . .

  e. The things I would not like in a small group are . . .

  f. What I hope for in this group is . . .

Option

Remember some invitations you have received—in person, by phone, or in the mail.

Think of one that you will never forget. Who invited you? To what? How did you feel?

Did you accept or refuse the invitation?

Opening prayer

Lord, we come with whatever faith, whatever understanding, whatever desire for you we have, trusting that because you have promised to hear us and love us, it is enough. Teach us to pray. Amen.

Ephesians 3:14-21

Read this passage silently; then listen to it read aloud slowly by one or two readers.

14 For this reason I bow my knees before the Father, 15from whom every family in heaven and on earth takes its name. 16I pray that, according to the riches of his glory, he may grant that you may be strengthened in your inner being with power through his Spirit, 17and that Christ may dwell in your hearts through faith, as you are being rooted and grounded in love. 18I pray that you may have the power to comprehend, with all the saints, what is the breadth and length and height and depth, 19and to know the love of Christ that surpasses knowledge, so that you may be filled with all the fullness of God.

20 Now to him who by the power at work within us is able to accomplish abundantly far more than all we can ask or imagine, 21to him be glory in the church and in Christ Jesus to all generations, forever and ever. Amen.

The many names of God

Andy has been in Alcoholics Anonymous for 12 years. He says, "I couldn't relate to the God they talked about in my church. In AA, they said it was okay to understand God in any way that helped me rely on God's power instead of mine. Now I've gone back to church. From my own experience I have a strong faith in God that I want to share with other people who need it too."

Have a different person read each of these four vignettes.

"I grew up in a small rural church," says Ardis, a young mother of three boys. "We had one of the best Sunday school teachers I've ever known. I've been careful ever since to make sure anything I believe about God can be found in the Bible. My relationship with God through Bible study and prayer has shaped my whole life."

Susan, a doctor, is straightforward. "I'm questioning and doubting God more than believing. Who can watch the news and believe in a God who is in control, or even cares? Jesus was poor, had compassion, spent his life for others. But God— where is God?"

"I have no teaching from childhood," says Bryce, vice president of a large bank. "My family never went to church. Now I have friends who are New Age, Catholic, Episcopalian, charismatic, and who knows what else. How can I possibly decide who God really is? Can anyone know the whole truth?"

■ With which of these people do you identify the most?

Many sections in this resource can be used for journaling as well as for discussion in the group.

Some people may need a few minutes to think and/or write before discussing.

Some questions could be used at home for further reflection. Encourage people to do whatever is best for them.

- Imagine you are praying for each of these people, the way Paul prayed for the Christians at Ephesus. What do you think each needs most? What do they already know of God?

- What we believe about God says far more about us than about God. Do you agree or disagree? Why?

It is evident from Ephesians 3:14-21 that Paul and the early Christians have experienced God and Christ as Father, Spirit, power, and boundless love. The writers of the Bible used many images for God, each of which reveals some aspect of God's character. The different ways of describing God reflect the writers' different experiences of God. The psalm writers alone used hundreds of images, such as "my rock," "my shield," "my fortress," "my delight," "my song."

In the New Testament, many of the words used for God describe Jesus, as well. Christians believe that the nature of God was revealed most clearly in the person of Jesus, so many images can be used for both.

Like the Bible writers, we respond to different aspects of God depending on our beliefs, experiences, and needs. Our images of God often change with time.

Ultimately, the reality that is God is beyond all words, concepts, or symbols. But as that reality makes itself known in our lives, we are given identity and purpose, hope and meaning. We become God's people.

Following is a list of many of the names for God:

Discuss where your ideas about God have come from.

Mystery	Merciful One	Higher Power
Father	All-powerful One	Lawgiver
Lord	Light	Way
Friend	Brother	Truth
Beloved	Savior	Center
Healer	Suffering Servant	Guide
Teacher	Unknown One	Eternal One
Creator	Spirit	Redeemer
Judge	Jesus Christ	Love
Mother	Bread	Fire
Shepherd	Word	Refuge
Comforter	Protector	King
Midwife	Life-giver	Wisdom

Are there other words you would add to this list?

- Put an X by the words that describe your concept of God, your beliefs about who God is.

- Circle the qualities that best describe your personal experience of God; that is, what God has done or been in your life.

- Are the words you have marked with an X different from the ones you have circled?

No matter how little we know about God for sure, the fact that we want to pray means we are already in a relationship with a God who loves us. Prayer begins with God and God has invited us all. We may know how and why God invites us, or we may be wondering. Either way, God is with us, in us, and everywhere else as we gather here.

■ Does it seem possible to you that God invited you here and wants your company?

Discovery

If this study theme is used for more than one small group session, introduce subsequent sessions with a "Community Builder" and "Opening Prayer" and end with "Wrap-up."

Expanding our images of God

You're not alone if you think of God as an old man in the sky or a blurry being out there somewhere. We often need help to move us beyond images that limit God, that keep us feeling disconnected and distant from God, or that do not help us to experience God in the modern world.

Look back at Paul's prayer in Ephesians 3:16, 17, and 20. All three verses stress the power of God, the risen living Christ, and the Holy Spirit *within* each Christian.

Thomas Keating, who teaches centering prayer to thousands of people every year, believes that God's presence is often experienced from within. Many people have been helped to pray by connecting with God at the center of their being, instead of "out there somewhere."

■ Go back to the list on page 13. Put the word *inner* next to any image of God where this would describe or expand your sense of how God works—*inner* teacher, *inner* wisdom, *inner* guide, and so forth. Add any images of your own that aren't on the list.

Share some of your ideas with the group.

■ Which of these images is most real and powerful for you at this time in your life?

It may be helpful to think of God less as "who" than as "when." While we cannot see God, we can see God's aftereffects, the difference God makes in a person's life.

■ How many ways can you describe God using the phrase "God is when . . ." or "God was when . . ."?

Discuss as a group.

■ In which of the following areas is God most real to you?

a. Ordinary events
b. The news
c. Friends and family
d. A small group
e. Within me
f. Out there somewhere
g. Holy Communion
h. Baptism
i. Christian fellowship

j. Nature
k. Silence
l. Art or music
m. The poor and neglected
n. My church
o. Bible
p. Beyond space and time
q. A sermon
r. Other

■ According to the following verses, is the God of the Bible a person?

You may wish to locate and mark these Bible passages in advance for the sake of time and convenience.

a. Job 9:11
b. Hebrews 11:27

c. 1 Timothy 6:16
d. John 1:18

■ What personal characteristics are described in the following verses?

a. Exodus 20:1
b. Ephesians 4:30
c. Psalm 147:4-5

d. John 5:17
e. 1 Thessalonians 1:9

Divide into small groups by choosing which of these three questions you would like to discuss.

When you gather together again, share any interesting insights you have gained.

■ Do some of the biblical images of God we have identified make it easier for you to pray? Are there some that make it more difficult?

■ If we relate only to images of God we feel comfortable with, is there danger of our creating the God we want? How can we let God be God?

■ What is your strongest, oldest image of God, which will always be helpful to you and probably never change? Do you know where it comes from?

Many people are struggling to find faith in a world where God seems to be absent or powerless against human violence and natural disaster.

Discuss as a group.

■ Why pray?

■ Is the God of the Bible still active in human history?

■ In the biblical accounts of God's action, is God depicted as always in control of everything?

A further look

Read 1 Corinthians 1:18-25 and 2 Corinthians 12:1-10.

■ How was the power of God revealed in the life of Jesus Christ different from the power we see in most human power struggles?

■ What strong convictions about prayer does Paul reveal in the second letter to the Corinthians?

When this candle appears, remember to refer to page 4 for help in leading the prayer exercise.

Discuss as a group.

For prayer together

Close your eyes. Picture television newscasting and the worst scene you remember from the last few months. . . . Is God there? . . . Where? . . . What does God look like? . . . What is God doing? . . . Is God saying anything? . . . If so, what? . . . Amen.

Consider this

"People frequently turn away from listening to the loving words that God is saying to them. It is too good to be true. So they either hear Jesus say negative things to them like *Sinner* . . . etc., or they go blank and hear him say nothing? They still have to discover the God of the New Testament, whose love for them is unconditional and infinite."

Anthony deMello, *Sadhana: A Way to God*
(St. Louis: The Institute of Jesuit Sources, 1979), 112.

Anthony deMello, who was a Jesuit priest in India, is known worldwide for his retreats, tapes, and books on prayer.

■ How do you respond to his observation?

■ Has your experience of Jesus included more judgment, more love, or "going blank and hearing him say nothing"?

16

For prayer together

Recall the presence of the risen Lord. . . "Wherever two or three are gathered, there am I in the midst of them." Tell Christ you believe he is here with you. . . .

**Allow time for partici-
pants to respond to the
prayer exercise.**

Reflect on the fact that God loves and accepts you just as you are now. You do not have to change . . . or get rid of all your sins . . . He wants you to grow, but you have his love and acceptance before you decide to change. . . . You have God's love and acceptance so that you may change, so that you may want to change, but you have it whether you want to change or not. . . . Take some time to reflect on whether you can believe this or not. . . .

Say something to Jesus in response. It can be very few words, or maybe no words. It is possible to communicate without words. . . . Amen.

**Allow time for personal
responses.**

We often bring our task-oriented mentality even into prayer, focusing on what we would like to do for Christ. The most important thing is to know that above all, God is love, and that we are loved. Actions will come as a response.

Adapted from *Sadhana: A Way to God* by Anthony deMello
(St. Louis: The Institute of Jesuit Sources, 1979), 112.

- ■ Look again at the prayer in Ephesians 3:14-21 and change the pronouns from *you* to *me*.

- ■ Write out the new prayer in your journal so that it is a prayer for yourself.

- ■ Then recite it slowly, out loud or to yourself

Adapted from *Prayer and Temperament* by Chester P. Michael and Marie C. Norrisey
(Charlottesville, Va.: The Open Door, Inc., 1984), 65.

Wrap-up

See page 10 in the introduction for a description of "Wrap-up."

Before you go, take time for the following:

- **Group ministry task**

- **Review**

- **Personal concerns and prayer concerns**

- **Closing prayers**

Ongoing prayer requests can be listed on page 61. See page 62 for suggested closing prayers.

Daily walk

Bible readings

Day 1
Romans 8:38-39

Day 2
Hebrews 11:6

Day 3
John 15:16-17

Day 4
Genesis 18:23-25

Day 5
Acts 17:27-28

Day 6
Ephesians 4:6

Day 7
Psalm 145:8

Thought for the journey

"The assurance of God's love is that no matter what demons and angels of our character and relationships we will confront in the future, we will be cared for with a loving kindness beyond our ability to imagine." *One Prayer at a Time,* F. Forrester Church and Terrence J. Mulry, ed. (New York: Macmillan, 1989), 27.

Prayer for the journey

"Pour out Your love and fullness upon those who honor Your name, that Your kingdom may come and Your will may be done among us, for Jesus' sake. Amen." From *Lutheran Book of Prayer* by J. W. Acker, copyright © 1970 Concordia Publishing House. Reprinted by permission, 34.

Verse for the journey

"And to know the love of Christ that surpasses knowledge, so that you may be filled with all the fullness of God" (Ephesians 3:19).

2 What Happens When We Pray?

Focus

The more we pray, the more we gain an understanding of prayer (what we are doing, what we might expect, how it affects us) and the easier it is to pray with confidence.

Community building

Rank these statements in order of their importance to you, from 9 as most important to 1 as least important.

Be as honest as you can and share only what you want—these answers do not have to be shared with the group.

■ Reflect on these statements about why you are here:

a. I sense the need for "something more" than I already have in my life.

b. I know people who pray and I'd like to be more like them in some ways.

c. I want to share my experiences of God with people who will understand.

d. I've been a church member for years, but still have a lot to learn about listening to God.

e. I have physical or mental health problems and want to know more about God's healing power.

f. Considering the condition the world is in, I wonder if God hears or answers prayers. But I'm willing to learn.

g. Our society seems seriously confused about right and wrong. I would like to know how prayer can help me make moral decisions.

Option

Think back over the time since this group last met.

Were there any images of God that stayed with you, or any ideas from the previous session that you thought more about?

h. I want to move ahead, use my gifts, become my best self. I'm wondering how prayer can help me.

i. I'm so grateful for what God has done for me that I want to praise and thank God.

■ Break into pairs and share some responses with each other. When you regather as a group, anyone who wants to can share responses or questions with the whole group.

Discovery

Matthew 6:7-15

7 "When you are praying, do not heap up empty phrases as the Gentiles do; for they think that they will be heard because of their many words. 8Do not be like them, for your Father knows what you need before you ask him.

9   "Pray, then, in this way:
  Our Father in heaven,
    hallowed be your name
10   Your kingdom come.
    Your will be done,
      on earth as it is in heaven.
11   Give us this day our daily bread.
12   And forgive us our debts,
      as we also have forgiven our debtors.
13   And do not bring us to the time of trial,
      but rescue us from the evil one.'

14 For if you forgive others their trespasses, your heavenly Father will also forgive you; 15but if you do not forgive others, neither will your Father forgive your trespasses."

What are we doing?

Discuss as a group.

■ If our images of God affect our prayer, how did Jesus' image of God as Father affect his prayer?

■ What seven things does Jesus ask for?

■ If our prayers reveal as much about us as about God, what do Jesus' requests reveal about him?

Consider this

Respond as a group.

Holly's fourteen-year-old son had been spending time with a boy quite different from his usual friends. Concerned about the relationship, but not wanting to forbid it, she prayed for the boy. The next day he was arrested for shoplifting, and is getting some of the help he needs. She said, "I pray from habit, and stuff like this happens, but why? What am I doing?"

■ How would you respond to Holly's questions?

What are we asking?

It is true that prayer is not a wish list and God is not a cosmic vending machine. On the other hand, the Lord's Prayer is a list of requests. We begin asking as children and go on asking our whole lives. Those who love us don't usually mind—it means that we trust them enough to ask. As we mature in the Christian life, we often learn to ask God more wisely. But asking for small things, asking most when we're in trouble, and asking unwisely never end, because we're human.

Asking is only one part of any relationship. We don't fall in love, form friendships, or even work with colleagues just to get things for ourselves, or get things done. In the same way, we don't "use" God. Things do get done, gifts are given back and forth. But the real commitment grows from intimacy— from sharing our lives, becoming more than we could alone. Prayer is the conversation in an intimate relationship with God. All else flows from that.

Asking for things is one kind of asking. Asking about things— seeking understanding, is another. Our conversation with God is part of the human search for truth. In gospel stories, Jesus often asks questions. He refuses to provide easy answers, which would take away the human responsibility to search for truth. Often there are no clear answers—only the wisdom and courage to live as well as we can with the questions.

Discuss as a group.

■ What fundamental question is being asked in each of the following passages? Try to answer some of these questions for yourself. The answers will never be complete; these questions last a lifetime.

You may wish to locate and mark these Bible passages in advance for the sake of time and convenience.

a. John 1:35-39
b. John 3:1-10
c. John 5:1-9
d. John 13:12-20
e. Mark 10:46-52

21

Some people say that prayer is trying to change God's mind, or persuade God to intervene. Others say prayer is not exactly like that, but something happens when we pray that doesn't when we don't. Still others believe God will act for the best regardless of our prayers.

Explore and relate. *Explore* in groups of three or four; then *relate* a brief summary to the entire group.

■ What do you think?

■ Which of the following are necessary before our prayer will have any effect?

    a. Strong faith that prayer works.

    b. A good and righteous life.

    c. A lot of knowledge about prayer.

    d. Praying enough, and every day.

    e. Using the right methods.

    f. Being sincere, really meaning it.

    g. Correct beliefs about God and prayer.

    h. Ability to clear the mind of all thoughts.

    i. Praying only for what couldn't possibly be against God's will.

    j. Praying in the right group.

Being and doing

One of the most important things we accomplish by praying is learning the value of being, versus doing. Be willing to waste time with God. Don't decide what will happen. Don't expect certain things. Be patient, aware, and open to surprises. It's possible to just relax and enjoy being with God.

Consider this

"Prayer is trying to let your life be open to the channels of God's love and purpose. That kind of opening of life, of keeping doors, windows, attitudes, your mind, and your heart open to God, is prayer."

James Lawson in *Questions of Faith: Contemporary Thinkers Respond,* Dolly K. Patterson, ed. (Philadelphia: Trinity Press International, 1990), 11.

When this candle appears, remember to refer to page 4 for help in leading the prayer exercise.

For prayer together

This is time to just be with God,—no agenda. Pray for the presence of the Holy Spirit, in your own way. . . . Give thanks that you are here. . . .

Now close your eyes and become aware of your breath, going in and out. . . . Think of the air you breathe as God's breath, God's Spirit, as the Hebrews did. . . . This Spirit is all around us. . . . Just rest for a few moments, aware of God around us, and in us, like the air we breathe. . . .

Discovery

Remember, if this study theme is used for more than one small group session, introduce subsequent sessions with "Community Building" and "Opening Prayer" and end with "Wrap-up."

Share insights when you gather with the whole group.

What is promised?

- ■ Divide into smaller groups, each taking one or two of the following passages to read.

  a. John 15:7-12   d. Matthew 6:33-34 (6:25-32)
  b. Philippians 4:4-9   e. John 14:1-6
  c. Matthew 18:15-20   f. 1 John 5:13-15

- ■ In the above passages, what is promised and what is required of the disciples?

- ■ How do these promises match your experience of the Christian life?

What does God do?

"We don't believe in prayer, but if there's anything we can do. . . ." "Whenever I'm not sure, I just ask the Lord and he tells me exactly what to do. . . ." Both comments assume something about what God does in response to prayer. Most of us are somewhere in between these extremes, and we often wonder, "What does God do?"

People often talk about "answers to prayer." Many people keep prayer journals to record their prayer requests and then the answers as they come. This keeps their faith strong and reminds them to be grateful for what God has done.

Often there are specific answers to specific requests, and we would do well to keep track of them and especially to thank God for them. But just as often there are vague, nearly unidentifiable "effects" of prayer. We often recognize these effects only by hindsight, or only partially, or only when someone else names them. We may wonder if they're connected to our prayer at all.

Our requests may also be unspecific, something like, "I commit this situation to God's loving care" or "It will be interesting to see what God does about this." Specific prayer is very natural, but people differ greatly about whether it is necessary or effective.

Results of prayer

Of all these possibilities, check which ones you have experienced as a result of prayer—either your own or someone else's or a church's prayer.

Divide into pairs and share with each other your responses to the list.

When the whole group gathers, let anyone who wishes to, share their insights.

a. Change in behavior
b. Change in lifestyle
c. Change in attitude toward other(s)
d. Affirmation of choices already made
e. Stronger connection to other(s)
f. Compassion for self or other(s)
g. Opportunity for right work
h. Involvement in social justice
i. Healing of mental or physical illness or addiction
j. Release of gifts and powers
k. Fruits of the Spirit (see Galatians 5:22-23)
l. Direction or guidance
m. Ability to wait for results
n. Gratitude
o. A new vision
p. Willingness to suffer
q. Serenity, peace of mind
r. Energy
s. Ability to let go and let God
t. Insight leading to action
u. Dramatic unmistakable answers
v. Forgiveness and forgetting of sin
w. Healing of a church community or family
x. Belonging, community
y. Change in negative thoughts or feelings
z. Protection, rescue from certain disaster
aa. Relaxing and enjoying life more
bb. Knowing I am loved and accepted
cc. Help or strength for difficult or frightening things
dd. More faith in God
ee. Freedom from temptation
ff. Awareness of sin
gg. Understanding of circumstances
hh. Clarification of options
ii. Other

■ Is there anything on this list you would like to experience and feel frustrated about?

■ Choose one thing that you marked on the list. Tell a story about yourself that illustrates why you marked that item.

Our requests

Answers depend on questions. What are we praying—that God will bless our efforts, or that we will become united to God and God's purposes?

God does respond to our prayer, but we can never know how, or when, or why the response will come. Our prayer can never control God's gifts, God's power, or God's grace. It just opens us to them.

Meanwhile, we support, love, and encourage each other, rejoice with those who rejoice, mourn with those who mourn. We can all become someone else's answer to prayer.

Allow time for thoughts and reflections from the group.

Consider this

"'Hallowed be your name, your kingdom come, your will be done on earth as it is in heaven.' In the Lord's Prayer, God and God's will are clearly the centers of gravity. The Lord's Prayer tells me that my life becomes significant when it gets drawn into God's purpose. Yes, I need the things this prayer asks for and God invites me to ask in faith for all of these. But in the Lord's Prayer, what is most important is the coming of God's kingdom. When that happens, all my needs and desires are satisfied."

Leonard J. VanderZee, *The Banner, March 7, 1994, 20-24.*

For prayer together

The following prayers don't have to be shared—just write a word or two in your journal to remind you of the prayers. Use the list on page 24 if that helps to identify a need. Individually choose one prayer for yourself, one prayer for someone you know, and one prayer for the group.

At this time, recall your prayer for yourself. . . . Recall your prayer for someone you know. . . . Recall your prayer for the group. . . . In the name of Jesus Christ, our Lord. . . . Amen.

Over the next week, try to pray these three short prayers whenever you think of them. This is not a test of God's "answers" or our skill in prayer. Our goal is to become praying people, and each time we remember to pray, we're doing just that.

Wrap-up

See pages 10 in the introduction for a description of "Wrap-up."

Before you go, take time for the following:

■ Group ministry task

■ Review

■ Personal concerns and prayer concerns

■ Closing prayers

Ongoing prayer requests can be listed on page 61. See page 62 for suggested closing prayers.

Daily walk

Bible readings

Day 1
Isaiah 30:19-22

Day 2
Matthew 18:19-20

Day 3
Philippians 3:12, 4:9

Day 4
Psalm 40:1-5

Day 5
Jeremiah 29:12-13

Day 6
1 John 1:9

Day 7
Mark 14:32-42

Thought for the journey

"Prayer is the discipline on the way to action that relinquishes control and seeks direction from another. Prayer is not the last and hopeless act when all else has failed, but the [preparation] for healing action." Loren Halvorson in *A Primer on Prayer*, Paul R. Sponheim, ed., copyright © 1988 Fortress Press, 103.

Prayer for the journey

"My prayers, my God, flow from what I am not; I think thy answers make me what I am."

George MacDonald (1824–1905) in *The HarperCollins Book of Prayers*, 237.

Verse for the journey

"Your kingdom come, your will be done" (Matthew 6:10).

3 Prayer for Busy Lives

Focus

Prayer can be a part of ordinary life, and ordinary life a part of prayer. We can use short and simple ways to pray throughout the day that connect us more deeply to God, ourselves, others, and all creation.

Community building

Discuss the following questions as a group.

- Did you say a prayer of thanks before meals when you were growing up? If so, describe it. Did you like doing that?

- If your family didn't pray together, do you remember being in homes where other families did? How did you feel?

- Are you a "morning person," an "evening person," or is some other time your best time of day?

- What is your low energy time, when everything looks the worst?

- Do you have set routines that are the same every day— like taking a shower, reading the paper, or watching the news?

Option

Was there a time during the last week when any of these experiences happened?

You sensed God's presence, in any form.

You talked to God.

You sensed God saying something to you.

You saw anything in your life from a different perspective.

You became aware of God's love for you.

Opening prayer

Lord, I believe that I am always in your presence, but help me be more aware of your presence day by day. Teach me to talk with you as with a trusted friend, and slowly open me to your transforming love. Amen.

Psalm 4:1-8

1 Answer me when I call, O God of my right!
   You gave me room when I was in distress.
   Be gracious to me, and hear my prayer.
2 How long, you people, shall my honor suffer shame?
   How long will you love vain words, and seek after lies?
3   But know that the LORD has set apart the faithful for
      himself;
   the LORD hears when I call to him.
4 When you are disturbed, do not sin;
   ponder it on your beds, and be silent.
5 Offer right sacrifices,
   and put your trust in the LORD
6 There are many who say,
      "O that we might see some good!
   Let the light of your face shine on us, O LORD!"
7 You have put gladness in my heart
   more than when their grain and wine abound.
8 I will both lie down and sleep in peace;
   for you alone, O LORD, make me lie down in safety.

Morning and evening prayer

The psalm writer includes many emotions and moods in this prayer—distress, need, sarcasm, gratitude, anxiety, joy, peace of mind. Prayer is not trying to be holy or pure before you talk to God—it's bringing your thoughts and feelings, as they are, to the one who cares most. And prayer is not a big task to add to an already busy life, but the way we discover what things are worth being busy about.

The Bible is full of references to morning and evening prayer, such as Psalm 5:3; Mark 1:29-39; as well as Psalm 4:8. At the beginning and the end of the day, we can often find a few minutes to be quiet and alone. The bed we wake up and go to sleep in is a good place to begin "pondering and being silent" (see Psalm 4:4).

Some of us may feel that there's no time for prayer in the morning. But even as we wake up, we can greet God and remind ourselves of God's presence. It really makes a difference if we ask for what we need most during the coming day before we step out into the world and the day's events begin.

Discuss as a group.

■ Which of these Bible verses identify what you need during an average day?

    a. "Worship the LORD with gladness; come into his presence with singing" (Psalm 100:2).

    b. "Set a guard over my mouth, O LORD; keep watch over the door of my lips" (Psalm 141:3).

    c. "Those who wait for the LORD shall renew their strength" (Isaiah 40:31).

    d. "Love your enemies and pray for those who persecute you" (Matthew 5:44)

    e. "When I sit in darkness, the LORD will be a light to me" (Micah 7:8).

    f. "You have received without payment; give without payment" (Matthew 10:8).

    g. "The LORD is my shepherd, I shall not want" (Psalm 23:1).

■ Why do you choose these particular Bible verses?

For prayer together

Find a comfortable position, in a chair or on the floor if you prefer. Think back over your day (today or yesterday)—what you did, what happened to you, what went well, and not so well. . . . Is there anything you wish you could do over? . . . . Ask for whatever you need: God's forgiveness, help in making it all right if that's possible, a way to do it differently next time. . . .

Did anything special happen, some experience affect you deeply? . . . God is hidden in the events of our lives. What might God have meant for you to discover today? . . .

Now "count your blessings". . . remembering the thing for which you are grateful. . . . Thank God for all of it, and for life itself. . . . There are many saying, "Oh, that we might see some good!" (Psalm 4:6). . . . Be one of those who recognizes good when you see it, and gives thanks. . . .

For prayer at home

Before we fall asleep, we usually think back over the day. Evening prayer is doing this with God, asking the Holy Spirit to show us what we may have missed in the busyness of the day. Try the following evening prayer at home before you go to sleep, either in bed or sitting quietly in a chair.

Now leave your day with God. It is over. Put your trust in the Lord, and be at peace. . . .Amen.

Luke 24:28-31, 35

28 As they came near the village to which they were going, he walked ahead as if he were going on. 29But they urged him strongly, saying, "Stay with us, because it is almost evening and the day is now nearly over." So he went in to stay with them. 30When he was at the table with them, he took bread, blessed and broke it, and gave it to them. 31Then their eyes were opened, and they recognized him; and he vanished from their sight. . . . 35Then they told what had happened on the road, and how he had been made known to them in the breaking of the bread.

Table prayers

People together, breaking and sharing bread, seeing in a new way. Jesus shared himself, as he has ever since, in the breaking of bread at the Last Supper. Here he reveals himself to the disciples at the evening meal on the first Easter Sunday.

We also are invited to share and reveal ourselves with those at our table. An evening meal may be the only time in the day or even in the week when the family is together.

Discuss as a group.

- How do we become known to each other at mealtime?

- How could we begin to see and hear in new ways?

- If you live alone, where and how do you experience community at meals?

- Do you say grace before meals at your house? If so, how do you do it? If not, what gets in the way?

It may not be easy to pray together as a family. No matter who is in your family right now, begin simply. Just give thanks for the food. "Lord God, thank you for giving us this food."

As time goes on, people might sometimes mention other things from their day.

From here, you could begin praying for others to have what they need, and for yourselves to find ways to share what you have.

- If there are children in your home, how might they benefit from hearing you pray?

Table graces

"Praise the LORD, O my soul, and do not forget all his benefits" (Psalm 103:2).

Here are a few examples of table prayers from *One Hundred Graces* (selected by Marcia and Jack Kelly. New York: Bell Tower, 1992).

a. Lord, bless our meal, and as you satisfy the needs of each of us, make us mindful of the needs of others.

Mount St. Mary's Abbey, Wrentham, Mass.

b. May God bless our meal and grant us a compassionate and understanding heart toward one another.

Mount St. Mary's Abbey, Wrentham, Mass.

c. God, I thank you for the blessings and gifts that You have provided for me and my relatives, and the food that you have provided also. I pray that we will receive strength and good health from it. So be it.

Lakota grace translated by Bill Quejas.

d. Give us this day our daily bread, O Father in heaven, and grant that we who are filled with good things from Your open hand may never close our hearts to the hungry, the homeless, and the poor; in the name of the Father, and of the Son, and of the Holy Spirit.

Abbey of New Clairvaux, Vina, Calif.

e. Let there be peace on earth and let it begin with me. Peace in our food, Peace in our bodies, Peace in our home, Peace in our world. Thanks, God. Amen.

The Rev. Dr. Barbara King,
Hillside International Truth Center, Atlanta, Ga.

You may wish to share your prayers with each other.

Write a short table prayer that you could use at home. It need not be like these; prayer is an honest expression of what you feel. If writing seems difficult, just make a list of the things you would include in your prayer.

Respond as a group.

Consider this

Dorothy Day, who devoted her life to helping the poor and homeless, said, "We cannot love God unless we love each other, and to love each other we must know each other in the breaking of bread and we are not alone any more. Heaven is a banquet and life is a banquet, too, even with a crust, where there is companionship. Loves comes with community."

One Hundred Graces, 107.

Luke 18:9-13

⁹ [Jesus] also told this parable to some who trusted in themselves that they were righteous and regarded others with contempt: ¹⁰ "Two men went up to the temple to pray, one a Pharisee and the other a tax collector. ¹¹The Pharisee, standing by himself, was praying thus, 'God, I thank you that I am not like other people: thieves, rogues, adulterers, or even like this tax collector. ¹²I fast twice a week; I give a tenth of all my income.' ¹³But the tax collector, standing far off, would not even look up to heaven, but was beating his breast and saying, 'God, be merciful to me, a sinner!'"

Breath prayers

"Lord Jesus Christ, Son of God, have mercy on me, a sinner."

We do not need to use a lot of words to inform God, impress others, or feel more spiritual. The tax collector used one short sentence. The Jesus Prayer, used in the early church, is a similar heartfelt request. . . . "Lord Jesus Christ, Son of God, have mercy on me, a sinner." At any time of the day or night, this ancient, simple prayer is being repeated by Christians all over the world. Many people pray it in rhythm with breathing— "Lord Jesus Christ" on the in breath, "have mercy on me" on the out breath. The prayer becomes a reminder of who we are as Christians—dependent on grace, trusting in God as ultimately merciful.

Discuss as a group.

In the New Testament, the word *mercy* means not only forgiveness, but also the outward acts arising from Jesus' compassion—feeding, teaching, healing.

- When you pray "have mercy on me," what compassionate gift of God might you be asking for right now?

For prayer together

Find a comfortable position where you are seated. . . . Close your eyes. . . . Breathe slowly a few times; . . . Then begin to repeat the Jesus Prayer ("Lord Jesus, Son of God, have mercy on me, a sinner.") as you breathe in and out. . . . If your mind wanders, gently come back to the prayer. . . .

After five minutes, quietly begin to pray together the Lord's Prayer.

- Have you ever sat silently in a group for this long? How did it feel?

- If you wish to, describe how the prayer went for you.

You will find many other breath prayers if you are watching for them. Certain words will seem to be "your" words to God, or God's words to you. Scripture, hymns, the liturgy, poetry, and songs are full of such phrases:

The mark / between words indicates the place to exhale.

Come, / Holy Spirit.
Now the silence, / now the peace.
Thy will be done, / not mine.
Thank you, / Jesus.
Into your hands, / commit my spirit.
Lord of life, / send my roots rain.

Have a hymnal available for each person.

Open the hymnal now, to a favorite hymn. There is probably a line that you especially like. Let the line condense into a shorter phrase if it's too long for a breath prayer. Close your eyes and pray the phrase, breathing slowly, for a few minutes, until the facilitator ends the time with a quiet "Amen."

Go back to page 13 for a list of various images of God.

You can create your own breath prayers. Choose a name or image of God and a deep personal need or desire. Combine them into one phrase. Here are examples of biblical images combined with personal needs:

    a. "Jesus healer, make me whole" (see Luke 4:38-41).
    b. "Loving mother, hold me close" (see Psalm 131:2).
    c. "Spirit of God give us peace" (see John 14:25-27).

Say your prayer during the day, whenever you think of it. This helps to bring about the renewing of the mind that Paul describes in Romans 12:2, "Do not be conformed to this world, but be transformed by the renewing of your minds."

Say your prayer while working on tasks that don't need your full attention, while waiting in a line or stuck in traffic, when your energy is low, or in times of confusion, depression, or grief when you don't know how else to pray.

There are many good guided prayer tapes available. You can listen to them in the car, walking, in bed at night— wherever you can take a small tape recorder and earphones.

Some are mostly teaching, others have more space for your own prayer. Christian bookstores, retreat houses, and people who already use tapes will help you find some that you like. Some are listed on page 62.

In the middle of the night, it is a good way to "turn off" a worried mind and "turn on" your trust in God. If you want to read the Bible, or do any other kind of prayer, breath prayers are a way to settle down and focus before you begin.

■ What do you think is the purpose of this type of prayer? Choose one or more and explain.

    a. To help you feel better.
    b. To connect consciously with God.
    c. To deal with your problems so you can use your energy for others.
    d. To be transformed in ways you may not imagine.

■ Do you know anyone who seems to have the new mind and new way of seeing that Romans 12:2 describes?

■ What do you know about how he or she prays? Take a risk and ask—you may have a discussion that will be very helpful to you.

Wrap-up

Before you go, take time for the following:

- Group ministry task

- Review

- Personal concerns and prayer concerns

- Closing prayers

Daily walk

Bible readings

Day 1
Psalm 5:3

Day 2
Psalm 141:2

Day 3
Psalm 119:148

Day 4
1 Corinthians 10:31

Day 5
1 Corinthians 10:17

Day 6
Psalm 71:8

Day 7
1 Thessalonians 5:16-18

Thought for the journey

"Who can spread his hours before him, saying, 'This is for God and this for myself; This for my soul and this other for my body?' . . . Your daily life is your temple and your religion."

The Prophet, by Kahlil Gibran
(New York: Alfred A. Knopf, 1923, 1951), 77-78.

Prayer for the journey

Dear Lord, open my eyes, that I may see. Incline my heart, that I may desire. Guide my steps, that I may walk in your way. Amen.

Verse for the journey

"Do not be conformed to this world, but be transformed by the renewing of your minds, so that you may discern what is the will of God—what is good and acceptable and perfect" (Romans 12:2).

4 How Do We Pray?

Focus

The kinds of prayer that are best for one person are not necessarily best for someone else. Discovering our own ways of praying and gathering with others to pray both nourish our relationship with God.

Community building

Record the first four directives (to the right) in advance on a tape and play for the "Community Building" exercise, or have a volunteer read them while others listen and follow.

- Close your eyes. . . . Take a few deep breaths. . . . Put aside all that you experienced today. . . . This is your time to pray. . . . Be here, now. . . .

- Remember Jesus' words, "Where two or three are gathered in my name, I am there among them" (Matthew 18:20).

- Now begin to say to yourself, "How blessed I am. How grateful I am." As you repeat these words, recall some of your life's blessings. . . .

- Go over in your mind all the events of yesterday or today. Be grateful for them. Say, "Thank you. How blessed I was, that that happened to me." When you come to an unpleasant event, consider the seeds for growth that it contains.

- Share with the group anything from this prayer that you choose, especially anything surprising.

Option

Did you have any further thoughts about last week's session?

Is there one of the prayer exercises that you would like to use to begin this time together?

Opening prayer

Lord, in the midst of our busy, noisy lives, we thank you for the blessing of quiet time with you and with each other. Amen.

Matthew 6:5-6

5 "Whenever you pray, do not be like the hypocrites; for they love to stand and pray in the synagogues and at the street corners, so that they may be seen by others. Truly I tell you, they have received their reward. 6But whenever you pray, go to your room and shut the door and pray to your Father who is in secret; and your Father who sees in secret will reward you."

Praying alone

Praying with other Christians was very important in the early Christian community. But Jesus also taught that we need time alone with God as well.

Prayer in small groups such as this one, in church services, and in other gatherings is easier for many people than praying alone. In groups, someone leads us. We do what the others do. Alone, we often wonder if we are praying "the right way" or "enough" or about "the right things."

Simple ways of praying that have been used by Christians for centuries may help us "draw near to God and let God draw near to us" (James 4:8).

Finding our best ways to pray may be less of a problem for many of us than finding our best time. Religion scholar Jacob Needleman has said that many Americans suffer from a "poverty of time." Almost all of us are very busy, but we can find a few minutes a day for prayer.

- Do you spend any time alone in an average week? Is any of that time quiet and uninterrupted?
- Is there a noticeable connection between how, or how much, you pray, and how your life goes?
- Is there one time in your day when you could spend 15 or 20 minutes praying?

At home

A free evening with no scheduled activities—a mini-retreat—is really helpful every so often.

Discuss who in the group has done this somewhat regularly.

- How have individuals taken time out from normal responsibilities for a free, peaceful evening?

If you live in a busy family with children, it can be difficult. If you're a single parent, an older child, babysitter, or friend with whom you can exchange responsibilities could give you an uninterrupted quiet evening. For couples, you and your spouse can exchange evenings, one cleans up after supper and, where applicable, gets everyone to bed, giving the other person free time.

Ways of praying

Explore and relate.

We can try many ways of praying, but the ones we stay with will need to fit us like comfortable old shoes. They will change as our lives and our personalities change, and as we grow older. Here are some suggested ways of praying.

a. Responding to a passage of Scripture
b. Journaling
c. Using prayers written by others
d. Singing hymns or songs
e. Looking at something in nature
f. Praying with a small group
g. Silent meditation
h. Guided prayer tapes
i. Listening to music
j. Praying in worship services
k. Responding to books other than the Bible
l. Praying with a partner
m. Prayer retreats
n. Praying as you walk or run
o. Other

Which of these ways of praying have you experienced?

- Which of these ways of praying have you exprienced?

- Which have you liked best? Stayed with longest?

- Which sounds like something new you would like to try?

- What can prayer involve besides words?

For prayer together

- Ask a volunteer to choose a favorite written prayer, possibly from one of the collections listed in the bibliography on page 62.

- Read this prayer aloud, as a group. Read it again slowly, to yourselves.

Written prayers may express what we want to say, or lead us into our own prayer. Use this prayer in any way you choose—whether you use one word, one phrase, or the whole prayer. Try speaking to God for awhile in your own words. Then just sit in silence and let God speak to you. . . .

Discuss rituals.

Consider this

The church has always used rituals and symbols. They are powerful, expressing God's love to us in ways that words alone cannot.

You can create your own rituals to do the same. Sally had some large medical bills to pay and was afraid there would be more. She happened to be playing a tape of some Russian Orthodox music. The sound of those huge beautiful chords and low basses suddenly made her realize, "God is much bigger than these bills." Since then, she often lights a candle and plays this music when paying bills—it reminds her that God's resources are greater than her own.

- **What is a powerful symbol for you—light, candles, incense, something in nature, certain music, something else?**

- **Where is it—church, your home, outdoors?**

- **What meaning does it convey to you?**

For prayer together

- Have someone place a special symbol—an icon, a candle, a rock, a bunch of flowers or leaves, or some other object—in the center of the group

- Look at this object. Don't look for anything sensational. Just look, as if you are seeing it for the first time.

If it says something to you about God, or your relationship with God, fine, but this isn't necessary. Just looking at the creation with enjoyment and attention is good. . . . Look for five or ten minutes without thinking much. . . . just observe. . . .

- Here are some possible ways to pray at home, at work, or in your car:

Share individual thoughts, preferences, or decisions with the group.

   a. Buy a daily devotional book. There are many kinds available. Each day, read the page for that day and write your response on the bottom of the page.

   b. Buy one or two good collections of prayers. Two are recommended on page 62, but there are many others. Browse until you find prayers that sound like what you would like to say. The book of Psalms in the Bible is the traditional prayer book of the Christian church.

Acts 2:42

⁴² They devoted themselves to the apostles' teaching and fellowship, to the breaking of bread and the prayers.

The church gathered

The prayer of the gathered church has always been the one way that all Christians prayed, regardless of personal differences. We learn what Christian prayer is (and is not) through participating in the liturgy. And most of us need the support. If we pray only when we feel like it, or really need it, we soon give up. We need other Christians and the structure of prayer together.

Praying the liturgy moves us beyond self-centeredness. When we pray with a church, we are no longer in control. Our individual feelings and needs are not central. With other people, some very different from us, our individual lives are directed to God's Word for us all, calling us outward to the needs of the whole world.

Each one of us is reminded that we do not stand alone, dependent on one's own changeable feelings or flickering faith. We are part of the concerns and commitments, the hopes and visions, the joys and struggles, of our brothers and sisters in God.

Discuss as a group.

■ How has the church, through worship or in other ways, helped teach you to pray?

■ How many kinds of prayers (times when the people speak directly to God) are there in the worship service?

We often notice those prayers that particularly reflect our own experience or concerns. When a prayer seems very odd and disconnected to your life, try to ask, "Who would pray this prayer?" For example, look at Psalm 31:12-15. Who might experience this? It might be people who are experiencing such oppression and fear because of political conflict, warfare, mental illness, or any other circumstance that causes this kind of misery.

■ Are there kinds of prayer that you would like to see added to public worship services? Explain.

Praying with others

Those who begin to value prayer more and more often seek others to pray with outside of the worship service. There are also many opportunities for good retreats on prayer.

You will probably discover that many of the kinds of prayer we are experiencing in this group are easier to do together than alone. It's helpful to find that everyone has similar questions and problems with praying. It's good to have a place to share what's happening in your life and how that connects with your praying. And (you may have noticed this) for some people, it's often easier to become quiet and focused in a group than when we are alone. The silence of the group becomes deeper and more silent than our own.

Place a candle in front of each person.

Choose a partner and find a place where you can talk without hearing others.

For prayer together

■ Take five minutes each. Describe what you are most grateful for, and how you most need God's help.

■ Pray in your own way, aloud or silently, about what your partner needs most. Then let your partner pray for you.

■ Come back together as a group. Take time to talk about anything you feel was significant in this experience.

■ Go around the group, each person lighting their candle and saying one brief thing about what the lighted candle symbolizes to them about people.

■ Take about five minutes and pray silently together the breath prayer: "I thank God / for all of you."

Discovery

Psalm 103:1-2

**1 Bless the LORD, O my soul,
and all that is within me,
bless his holy name.
2 Bless the LORD, O my soul, and
do not forget all his benefits.**

Praise and thanksgiving

Thanksgiving is gratitude for God's gifts, and praise is gratitude for God's being who God is. If people who are experienced in prayer agree on anything, it is that the more grateful we are for what we have been given, the more open we are to receive God's gifts. There is no sweeter prayer on earth than a grateful heart.

Discuss as a group.

■ Name some people who regularly thank you for what you do for them, or give them.

- Name some who praise you—who tell you how grateful they are just because you are you.

- Who or what do you think receives praise in our culture?

a. Sports teams	g. Consumer products
b. Music groups	h. Scientists
c. Cars	i. Teachers
d. Technology	j. Children
e. Parents	k. Religious leaders
f. Movie stars	l. Other

For prayer together

- Create a litany, together as a group, by choosing five or six reasons to thank and five or six reasons to praise God.

  For _____, we give you thanks, O Lord.

  For _____, we praise you, O God.

- When you are done, pray the litany together.

Share your litany with worship leaders and ask them to consider using it in a Sunday worship service.

Music and prayer

Tom tells this story: "My family and I recently moved from a town where I was in three, sometimes four singing groups, and suddenly I was not singing at all. After a few months of feeling heavy in spirit and disconnected from God, I realized how much of my prayer is in the form of song."

Music, in its many varieties, has always played a large part in Christian worship. Many hymns and songs are really prayers, and the psalms were meant to be sung—they are the hymn book of the Bible. There's something about throwing our whole self—body, voice, and mind—into a song that gets us out of ourselves and totally focused on what we are singing. Music also unites us. Whatever differences we may bring to a choir, or to a congregation, when we begin singing we are one.

Each person will need a hymnal.

- Look in the index of the hymnal and find three or four of your favorite hymns or titles that simply attract your attention. Choose one that is a prayer, one that speaks directly to God. Read through the text and notice which lines express things that are important to you.

- If there are enough people in the group who like to sing, sing the favorite stanza of everyone's hymn.

Listening to music can be a way into prayer just as Bible reading or breath prayers or any other way of focusing our attention.

Option

Choose a short (three- to five-minute) piece of recorded Christian music that you think the group will enjoy and be prepared to play it for the group.

- How has music been part of your spiritual life? (Tapes, choirs, instruments, church, concerts, singing, playing, listening, other.)

Wrap-up

Before you go, take time for the following:

- Group ministry task

- Review

- Personal concerns and prayer concerns

- Closing prayers

Daily walk

Bible readings

Day 1
Romans 8:26

Day 2
1 Thessalonians 5:16-18

Day 3
1 Timothy 2:1

Day 4
Mark 1:35, 45

Day 5
John 6:15

Day 6
Ephesians 5:19-20

Day 7
Psalm 145:18

Thought for the journey

"[C]ommon prayer is precious and the most powerful, and it is for its sake that we come together . . . the Christian church on earth has no greater power or work against everything that may oppose it than such common prayer"

Martin Luther in "Treatise on Good Works."

Prayer for the journey

Lord, lead me to those with whom I can pray, and those who need me to pray with them. Amen.

Verse for the journey

"They devoted themselves to the apostles' teaching and fellowship, to the breaking of bread and the prayers" (Acts 2:42).

5 Intercession: Praying for Others

Focus

Intercession happens any time we bring anyone to Jesus and ask for his Spirit to be with them. When we do this, we become ministers who connect those we love to God.

Community building

We read together; then take a time of silence for particular concerns.

In the center, place an assortment of pictures, newspaper and magazine headlines, flowers, lit candles, and any other objects that remind you of the needs of the world.

> *O Gentle Healer,*
> *I bring to you this night*
> *The joys and fears,*
> *Secrets and dreams of this day.*
>
> *I bring my family and friends,*
> *Neighbors and coworkers,*
> *My enemies, my rivals,*
> *The ones I cannot forgive.*
>
> *I bring you the poor and needy,*
> *The war-torn and oppressed,*
> *The abused and forgotten,*
> *The lonely and the lost.*

- In silence, let each of us offer prayers for ourselves, others, and creation, being sensitive to particular hopes, concerns, joys, and sadnesses of this day or week.

- Pray your prayers in silence. To conclude, one person says on behalf of all, ". . . through Jesus Christ our Lord." All others say, "Amen."

- Share what the prayer exercise was like for you. Did it lead to a serene feeling or even a lighter moment?

Option

Did you try any of the ways of praying from chapter 4?

If so, how did it go?

Discovery

Mark 2:1-12

[1] When he returned to Capernaum after some days, it was reported that he was at home. [2] So many gathered around that there was no longer room for them, not even in front of the door; and he was speaking the word to them. [3] Then some people came, bringing to him a paralyzed man, carried by four of them. [4] And when they could not bring him to Jesus because of the crowd, they removed the roof above him; and after having dug through it, they let down the mat on which the paralytic lay. [5] When Jesus saw their faith, he said to the paralytic, "Son, your sins are forgiven." [6] Now some of the scribes were sitting there, questioning in their hearts, [7] "Why does this fellow speak this way? It is blasphemy! Who can forgive sins but God alone?" [8] At once Jesus perceived in his spirit that they were discussing these questions among themselves; and he said to them, "Why do you raise such questions in your hearts? [9] Which is easier, to say to the paralytic, 'Your sins are forgiven,' or to say 'Stand up and take your mat, and walk'? [10] But so that you may know that the Son of Man has authority on earth to forgive sins"—he said to the paralytic—[11] "I say to you, stand up, take your mat, and go to your home." [12] And he stood up, and immediaately took the mat and went out before all of them; so that they were all amazed and glorified God, saying, "We have never seen anything like this!"

Questions about intercessory prayer

One way to let Bible stories become alive and real to us is by projecting ourselves back into the events and becoming part of them.

- ■ Take a few minutes to imagine the different viewpoints of the people who were there—the paralyzed man, his friends, the owner of the house, the ordinary people Jesus was talking to when the interruption occurred, the scribes, and Jesus himself. . . .

■ Now choose one of these characters, whichever one interests you most. What is he or she seeing and hearing from his or her viewpoint? Where is this person? What does he or she touch, and do, and say, as the story unfolds? Why does this person do and say this?

■ Now tell the story as a group by having each actor in the event tell about his or her experience. It may turn out that not all are represented. Add anyone who is missing at the end, if you want to.

Just like the people in Mark 2:1-12, our understanding of God, the Bible, human psychology, medical science, and many other factors influence our beliefs about prayer for other people—called intercessory prayer.

■ Which of the following can you easily agree or disagree with? Which do you have questions about?

Put yes or no or question marks in front of each statement. Then discuss as a group.

a. We should pray for God's will and leave it at that.

b. Prayer is more effective if you are with the person you are praying for.

c. Prayer helps the one praying more than the one prayed for.

d. I must feel very positive about the outcome if I am to pray effectively.

e. Some people have a special gift for intercessory prayer.

f. Prayer is a last resort when all else has failed.

g. It is wrong to pray for someone who has not asked you to.

h. I have to be willing to get involved if I pray.

i. The ability to pray effectively for others can be acquired.

j. God's will is always for healing and wholeness, and God will intervene without our asking.

k. It makes no sense to pray for "our side" in things like sports, or wars, or elections when others are praying for "their side."

l. My prayer can help someone who has no faith of their own.

m. It is good to ask God to show me specific needs and pray for them.

n. Most healings are a coincidence.

o. Prayer is unreliable.

■ Look back at the parable of the paralyzed man. What does this story seem to say about some of these issues?

Discovery

1 Timothy 2:1-4

[1] First of all, then, I urge that supplications, prayers, intercessions, and thanksgivings be made for everyone, [2] for kings and all who are in high positions, so that we may lead a quiet and peaceable life in all godliness and dignity. [3] This is right and is acceptable in the sight of God our Savior, [4] who desires everyone to be saved and to come to the knowledge of the truth.

Sharing God's work

As Christians, we are baptized into a community of faith that shows love by praying for those in need. Our prayers can easily tend toward, "God, listen to me, give to me," but as we become aware of the needs of others we also pray, "God, give through me. . . . "

In some way—and no one understands this very well—we become a point of contact, a channel for Christ's activity that would not be there without us and our prayer. Prayer opens us to God and others, especially to the suffering of the world—to the pain of those who cause it and those who experience it. We begin to want to respond in some way, even though we can't solve or even understand the problem. Prayer makes us available as one way that God can reach, save, and bless people. We may be used directly, or indirectly, but we find ourselves becoming willing, through our prayer, to become part of the answer. We become partners in God's work. Our desire to pray for others and our faith increases as we see our prayer make a difference.

How should we pray? People disagree. Many experienced pray-ers say they become less and less specific, praying only for what is best for the person and to be shown their own role, if any. Other people seek to know what they should pray for, and then pray for quite specific results. Often we find ourselves moving from specific requests to acceptance, watching for indications of what God might be doing. Ultimately, intercession is inviting God to work in a person or situation in God's way, not ours.

There are many passages in the Bible about giving thanks in all circumstances, even the most difficult. As Wendell Berry said, "Be joyful, though you have considered all the facts."

■ Look at:

Discuss as a group.

    a. Philippians 4:5-6   c. Matthew 6:25-34
    b. Psalm 30:4-5   d. 1 Thessalonians 5:16-18

■ Is this attitude realistic? Has there ever been a time when you were able to do this?

■ Why is it important in praying for others?

What we say and how we say it may matter very little. Simple breath prayers, such as "Jesus healer, make her whole," are especially easy to remember. We may use no words at all, and have only an image, a picture in our mind of what we are praying for. What seems to matter most is bringing the person or situation to Jesus for healing just as the paralyzed man's friends brought him. Hold them together in your mind. "Jesus, healer—Paul, my son. Jesus—Paul. Jesus—Paul." Some people find it easy to visualize Jesus with the person in need, others do not. It doesn't matter. According to divine promise, God knows, cares, and loves. Let your prayer be simple and from the heart.

No matter whom we are praying for, some things are always the right thing to ask: that the person be delivered from evil, enfolded in God's love, and assured they are forgiven; however things go, they (and we) serve God and are filled with the Holy Spirit.

For prayer together

The Jesus Prayer, which we learned earlier (page 32), is one of the simplest ways to pray for someone, especially if we are tired or afraid or have no idea what, except God's grace, is needed.

    Lord Jesus Christ, / have mercy on her (or a name)
    Lord Jesus Christ, / have mercy on them.

■ For now, think of one person who needs your prayer. Close your eyes, and pray this breath prayer silently with the group, for five or ten minutes. Notice how powerful and how comforting it is to be with others who are bringing their loved ones to God.

■ According to the following verses, who are some people who may need our prayers?

Respond as a group.

    a. 1 Timothy 2:1-2   d. James 5:14
    b. Ephesians 1:16; 6:18 e. Matthew 5:44
    c. 2 Corinthians 1:11   f. Acts 12:5

Dietrich Bonhoeffer in his classic book, *Life Together,* said, "We cannot hate the brother for whom we pray."

- Is there someone for whom you feel resentment, anger, even hatred, for whom you could try praying instead? *Note: This does not mean staying around abusive people. Some people are best prayed for from a distance. But prayer can help to bring healing even into very difficult relationships.*

- Who are some people outside the circle of those you know that you have prayed for, and how did you come to do that?

- During worship from now on notice who, outside the church's membership, is included in the prayers.

Discovery

Romans 8:26

26 Likewise, the Spirit helps us in our weakness; for we do not know how to pray as we ought, but that very Spirit intercedes with sighs too deep for words.

Respond as a group.

Consider this

"God cannot want for us what is not possible. When we are as personalities, so reduced that we cannot entertain the thoughts and intuitions of faith and love, God no longer wants his will done by us, he wants it done for us by others." From *Five for Sorrow, Ten for Joy* by J. Neville Ward, copyright © Epworth Press. Reprinted by permission.

When we need prayer

There are times when we feel we can't pray, even if we want to. Despair, desperation, and the sense of being forsaken by God can become overwhelming. It is especially at these times we appreciate the Bible's comforting words in Romans 8:26.

We need people to intercede for us, too, and they are there if we are willing to admit how helpless we are. Asking someone to pray for us can feel scary and embarrassing. The rugged individualism of our culture has affected prayer. Most of us believe we should be able to take care of ourselves, that if we don't know how to pray right, we should be ashamed. But there are people who are willing to pray for you. Especially if you are in immediate need, find them. At some point, the paralyzed man had to let his friends pick up the bed and start walking.

For prayer together

Return to the original story on page 44. Imagine that you, as the personality you now are—not a Bible story character—are one of the friends who carry the paralyzed man to Jesus. . . .

■ Think of the person you have worried about most lately. Imagine that he or she is the one you are carrying.

    a. Did this person ask you to take him or her for healing, or did you and the others insist that he or she go? . . .

    b. How do you feel? What do you say on the way?

    c. How does your loved one look, lying there helpless?

    d. How does your loved one seem to feel about this?

    e. What do you hope for most?

    f. Can you leave it up to your friend and Jesus what happens between them?

■ Share with the group anything you think is significant for you about this prayer exercise.

As with other kinds of prayer, some people find this easy and others difficult. How we pray depends somewhat on personality, and it's normal to enjoy some kinds of prayer and find others to be nearly impossible.

Ask a volunteer to read this prayer aloud with pauses after each petition for participants to silently name those people in their hearts.

O God of love, we pray for love,
Love in our thinking, love in our speaking,
Love in our doing,
And love in the hidden places of our souls;
Love of our neighbors near and far;
Love of our friends old and new;
Love of those with whom we find it hard to get along;
And love of those who find it hard to get along with us;
Love of those with whom we work;
And love of those with whom we spend our leisure time;
Love in joy, love in sorrow;
Love in life and love in death
So that at last we may be ready to live with you,
Who are eternal love.

Adapted from *A Book of School Worship* by Willliam Temple, copyright © Macmillan and Company Ltd. Reprinted by permission.

Conversation can become prayer. When you recognize someone's deep need or desire, bring it to God for them in your prayers.

■ Add intercessions to your table prayers at home. They can be very short and simple. Teach children just to think of God or Jesus together with the person for whom you pray. That's enough. God knows the real need anyway.

Wrap-up

Before you go, take time for the following:

- Group ministry task

- Review

- Personal concerns and prayer concerns

- Closing prayers

Daily walk

Bible readings

Day 1
1 Samuel 2:1-10

Day 2
Luke 22:31-32

Day 3
Luke 1:46-55

Day 4
1 Thessalonians 1:2-3

Day 5
Ephesians 1:16-19

Day 6
John 17:9

Day 7
Philippians 1:3-6

Thought for the journey

"It is only at the end of this world that we shall realize how the destinies of persons and nations have been shaped . . . by the quiet, silent, irresistible prayer of persons the world will never know." *Sadhana: A Way to God* by Anthony deMello, (St. Louis: The Institute of Jesuit Sources, 1979), 118.

Prayer for the journey

"And this is my prayer, that your love may overflow more and more with true knowledge and full insight to help you determine what is best, so that in the day of Christ you may by pure and blameless" (Philippians 1:9-10).

Verse for the week

"They were all amazed and glorified God, saying, "We have never seen anything like this!" (Mark 2:12).

6 Don't Be Afraid to Ask, to Listen

Focus

If we are really honest, prayer can change the way we live our lives. If we learn to listen, God can be honest with us.

Community building

Most groups state their goals and expectations at the beginning. We have been trying to overcome the idea of prayer as task-oriented, something we can "use" to accomplish our goals. Instead, we have seen prayer more as being open to who God is, who we are, how God guides and transforms and loves us.

In that spirit, we are working on our goals at the end.

- What has happened for us, as a group? What have our goals turned out to be?

- Did your experience differ from what you expected?

- Have any of your personal goals and expectations about prayer been affirmed, strengthened, changed, or abandoned in these weeks of meeting together?

- What has surprised you most?

Option

Choose, as a group, one of your favorite prayer exercises from the whole course, and use it to begin this time together.

Opening prayer

"I no longer want just to hear about you, beloved Lord, through messengers. I no longer want to hear doctrines about you, nor to have my emotions stirred by people speaking of you. I yearn for your presence." Amen.

St. John of the Cross in *The Harper Collins Book of Prayers*, 213.

Luke 11:5-13

⁵ And he said to them, "Suppose one of you has a friend and you go to him at midnight and say to him, 'Friend, lend me three loaves of bread; ⁶for a friend of mine has arrived and I have nothing to set before him.' ⁷And he answers from within, 'Do not bother me; the door has already been locked, and my children are with me in bed; I cannot get up and give you anything.' ⁸ I tell you, even though he will not get up and give him anything because he is his friend, at least because of his persistence he will get up and give him whatever he needs.

⁹ "So I say to you, Ask, and it will be given to you; search, and you will find; knock, and the door will be opened for you. ¹⁰For everyone who asks receives, and everyone who searches finds, and for everyone who knocks, the door will be opened.¹¹Is there anyone among you who, if your child asks for a fish, will give a snake instead of a fish? ¹²Or if the child asks for an egg, will give a scorpion? ¹³If you, then, who are evil, know how to give good gifts to your children, how much more will the heavenly Father give the Holy Spirit to those who ask him!"

Asking

The Bible's writers on prayer suggest at every turn that we will be changed if we pray, if we are open to God. But they never suggest that we come to God in prayer with anything other than an honest expression of who we are and what we need.

Contemporary psychology has made us more aware that denying or rejecting parts of ourselves does not lead to wholeness, or to healing. So it is with God—prayer is the real conversation of the real self with God.

Discuss as a group.

■ Does Luke, in these verses, imply that we will get anything we want from God, if we only ask?

■ What do these verses tell us to do?

■ What do these verses promise we will receive?

Respond to this exercise as a group.

Ordinary things

Prayer has been called "the education of desire." We often begin praying about ordinary things, and we might as well, because they are important, too. But Jesus did say that God knows what we need even before we ask.

So why are we asking? Because the more we ask, the more we begin to understand what we really need. Such gifts of God as God's nearness, God's peace, the guarding of our hearts and minds, the Holy Spirit, may seem beyond us, more "religious" than we really feel. Health, long life, money, approval, a good job, a loving partner, may be much closer to what we have in mind.

Often we do get these things. But mainly, our desires change. We begin to really want what God wants. We begin to be really "transformed by the renewing of [our] minds" (Romans 12:2) so that the whole world looks different. We don't have to worry so much about what to pray for. In many situations, we simply pray that God's kingdom come, God's will be done, and to know our part in that.

Discuss as a group.

- Do you want your mind transformed, your desires changed? Or do you want to be free to want what other people have?

- Can you think of any way in which your desires have changed because you have prayed?

For prayer together

The psalm writers of the Bible asked God for things all the time. They often prayed something like this:

    a. God you are . . .

    b. In the past you have . . .

    c. Here is what I have done wrong . . .
       (or) is not going well . . .
       (or) is worrying me . . .

    d. Here is what I need. . . .

    e. Here is what I hope you can do. . . .

    f. Please don't do . . .

    g. Here is what I will do differently. . . .

    h. I have confidence in you, God. I know this will all turn out well, maybe look like this. . . . Then . . .

These will not be shared with the group, so be as honest as you can.

- Using the above form, write a psalm of your own. Take the time you need so you can express your needs and desires.

- At home, use this form and your journal to write psalms that reflect the different aspects of your life, just as the psalmists did.

Psalm 46:10

¹⁰ "Be still and know that I am God!"

Listening

Probably the hardest part of listening prayer for all of us is *giving up the need to "do something."* We are so used to being active and accomplishing things, that we fear that trying to listen to God is a waste of time, or at least is too slow. It's not efficient.

Another reason for being afraid to listen is because of *what we might hear.* There are all those needs out there. God might demand something of us beyond what makes sense, and already we're too busy.

Others of us are *afraid we won't hear a thing.* We'll try prayer and it won't work.

> ■ Which of the three reasons above has made it hard for you to listen to God?

The truth is, God is trying to communicate with us all the time through everything in our lives. Thomas Keating, who teaches centering prayer to thousands of people each year, has said, "We need good ways to close our mouths. God has been listening to us for years."

Even when we stop running around and close our mouths, the intellectual and emotional noise in our heads doesn't stop. Learning ways to quiet this incessant self-talk is not to achieve an empty mind, but to make some space where we can hear God.

Lectio divina

One of the best ways of hearing God speak is called *lectio divina* (lek'tsee oh di vee'na) or divine reading. This is using a passage of the Bible for prayer, rather than for study or ordinary reading. The book of Psalms and the four Gospels are good sources of texts for this type of prayer.

For prayer together

For this prayer exercise, select a Bible passage such as Psalm 139. Together, go through the directions below. For this kind of prayer it is ideal to have at least 30 minutes. For now, spend as much time as you have available.

Ask for a listening heart, that you may hear the word God wants to speak directly to you. Ask for the Holy Spirit to guide and lead you.

■ **Reading the Word**

   a. Read the passage slowly.

   b. Be aware of particular words, phrases, or sentences that attract you in a special way.

   c. Underline them or write them down.

■ **Pondering the Word**

   a. Stay with the part that most attracts you.

   b. Tell God why you find this word meaningful.

   c. How does it relate to your life?

■ **Praying the Word**

   a. Become aware of what God is saying to you in this Word.

   b. This does not always involve words.

   c. It can be an image, a brief thought, a feeling, an insight, a sense of God's presence or love, a desire to do something.

■ **Resting in the Word**

   a. Be silent for awhile.

   b. Rest in God's presence, in and around you.

   c. Then express (in writing, if you wish) what you experienced and how you feel.

■ **Living the Word**

   a. If the Word makes you want to do something, what is it?

b. True prayer ultimately results in action. But it's important to learn to listen to God without getting right back into applications and resolutions—in other words "accomplishing something."

c. Many times we will not see anything happening, but God's grace is at work in us.

At home

You can use these guidelines when you want to pray your Bible at home. Change the process in any way that makes it better for you.

Teach me to listen, Lord

End the course with the following prayer. Have a volunteer read the prayer aloud slowly . . . as others listen and pray silently.

> *Teach me to listen, Lord,*
> *to those nearest me,*
> *my family, my friends, my coworkers.*
> *Help me to be aware that*
> *no matter what words I hear, the message is,*
> *"Accept the person I am. Listen to me."*
>
> *Teach me to listen, Lord,*
> *to those far from me—*
> *the whisper of the hopeless,*
> *the pleas of the forgotten,*
> *the cry of the anguished.*
>
> *Teach me to listen, Lord,*
> *to myself.*
> *Help me to be less afraid,*
> *to trust the voice inside—*
> *in the deepest part of me.*
>
> *Teach me to listen, Lord,*
> *for your voice—*
> *in busyness and in boredom,*
> *in certainty and in doubt,*
> *in noise and in silence.*
>
> *Teach me, Lord, to listen.*
>
> *Amen.*

Wrap-up

Before you go, take time for the following:

- ■ Group ministry task

- ■ Review

- ■ Personal concerns and prayer concerns

- ■ Closing prayers

Daily walk

Bible readings

Day 1
Isaiah 29:13-14

Day 2
Psalm 107:1-9

Day 3
Psalm 19:14

Day 4
Psalm 62:5-8

Day 5
Matthew 19:16-26

Day 6
Philippians 4:8

Day 7
Proverbs 2:3-5

Thought for the journey

"It is not necessary to maintain a conversation when you are in the presence of God. We can come into his presence and rest our weary souls in quiet." O. Hallesby in *Bible Readings on Prayer* by Ron Klug, copyright © 1986 Augsburg Publishing House, 29.

Prayer for the journey

"Lord, as I read your words, let me hear you speaking. As I reflect on each page, let me see your image. And as I seek to put your precepts into practice, let my heart be filled with joy." Amen. Gregory of Nazianzus (329-289) in *The HarperCollins Book of Prayers*, 177.

Verse for the journey

"And the peace of God, which surpasses all understanding, will guard your hearts and your minds in Christ Jesus" (Philippians 4:7).

Appendix

Record information about group members here.

Names   **Addresses**   **Phone Numbers**

_____

_____

_____

_____

_____

_____

_____

_____

_____

Group commitments

"Do not be conformed to this world, but be transformed by the renewing of your minds, so that you may discern what is the will of God—what is good and acceptable and perfect" (Romans 12:2).

■ For our time together, we have made the following commitments to each other

■ Goals for our study of this topic are

■ Our group ministry task is

■ My personal action plan is

Prayer requests

Prayers

■ Closing Prayer

Lord God, you have called your servants
to ventures of which we cannot see the
ending, by paths as yet untrodden,
through perils unknown. Give us faith to
go out with good courage, not knowing
where we go, but only that your hand is
leading us and your love supporting us;
through Jesus Christ our Lord. Amen.

Lutheran Book of Worship, copyright © 1978, 153.

■ The Lord's Prayer

(If you plan to use the Lord's Prayer, record the version
your group uses in the next column.)

Resources

■ Books

Appleton, George, ed. *Oxford Book of
Prayer.* New York: Oxford Univ. Press,
1989.

Church, F. Forrester and Terrence J. Mulry,
ed.. *One Prayer at a Time.* New York:
Macmillan, 1989.

deMello, Anthony. *Sadhana: A Way to God.*
St. Louis: The Institute of Jesuit Sources,
1979.

Van deWeyer, Robert, comp. *The Harper-
Collins Book of Prayers: A Treasury of
Prayers through the Ages.* New York:
HarperCollins, 1994.

■ Audiocassette tapes

deMello, Anthony. *Wellsprings.* We and
God Spirituality Center, Jesuit Hall,
St. Louis, Mo.

Chittister, Joan. *Psalm Meditations.* Cre-
dence Cassettes, Kansas City, Mo.
Vol. 1–AA2122; Vol. 2–AA2123;
Vol. 3–AA2238; Vol. 4–AA2239;
Vol. 5–AA2389; Vol. 6–AA2390.

Wuellner, Flora Slosson. *Depth Healing and
Renewal through Christ.* The Upper
Room, Nashville. Tenn. UR664.

Please tell us about your experience with INTERSECTIONS.

4. What I like best about my INTERSECTIONS experience is

5. Three things I want to see the same in future INTERSECTIONS books are

6. Three things I might change in future INTERSECTIONS books are

7. Topics I would like developed for new INTERSECTIONS books are

8. Our group had _____ sessions for the six chapters of this book

9. Other comments I have about INTERSECTIONS are

Thank you for taking the time to fill out and return this questionnaire.

---------------------------FOLD CARD IN HERE, SEAL WITH TAPE, AND MAIL TODAY!---------------------------

Please check the INTERSECTIONS book you are evaluating.

☐ Following Jesus   ☐ Death and Grief   ☐ Men and Women
☐ The Bible and Life   ☐ Divorce   ☐ Peace
☐ Captive and Free   ☐ Faith   ☐ Praying
☐ Caring and Community   ☐ Jesus: Divine and Human   ☐ Self-Esteem

Please tell us about your small group.

1. Our group had an average attendance of _____ .

2. Our group was made up of
Young adults (19-25 years)
_____ Adults (most between 25-45 years)
_____ Adults (most between 45-60 years)
_____ Adults (most between 60-75 years)
_____ Adults (most 75 and over)
_____ Adults (wide mix of ages)
_____ Men (number) and _____ women (number)

3. Our group (answer as many as apply)
_____ came together for the sole purpose of studying this INTERSECTIONS book.
_____ has decided to study another INTERSECTIONS book.
_____ is an ongoing Sunday school group.
_____ met at a time other than Sunday morning.
_____ had only one facilitator for this study.

BUSINESS REPLY MAIL

FIRST-CLASS MAIL　　　PERMIT NO. 22120　　　MINNEAPOLIS, MN

POSTAGE WILL BE PAID BY ADDRESSEE

Augsburg Fortress

ATTN INTERSECTIONS TEAM
PO BOX 1209
MINNEAPOLIS MN 55440-8807